Original title:

Tarnished Pips Inside the Dragon Holt

Copyright © 2025 Swan Charm

Author: Sara Säde

ISBN HARDBACK: 978-1-80562-898-9

ISBN PAPERBACK: 978-1-80564-419-4

A Dance with Dusk's Remains

As shadows stretch in twilight's grace,
The stars prepare to find their place.
A whispering wind, soft and light,
Invites the moon to join the night.

In the garden, dreams take flight,
With petals closed, yet hearts so bright.
The fireflies weave through the air,
Painting magic, sweet and rare.

Beneath the arches of fading light,
Where secrets stir and take to flight,
The world, adorned in velvet hues,
Sings softly of forgotten views.

A reverie calls from deep within,
Where hopes revive and life begins.
With every breath, the dusk compels,
A chorus rich, where silence dwells.

As night enfolds the weary day,
The heart finds peace in shadows' play.
A dance unfolds with gentle ease,
In the embrace of twilight's breeze.

The Echoing Pulse of Secrets

In shadows deep, the whispers swell,
A tale of magic, lost to tell.
Through moonlit paths, the secrets glide,
Each echo carries hopes that bide.

The stars above, they know our plight,
Entwined in dreams that spark the night.
From every corner, voices rise,
A pulse that dances through the skies.

In silence bound, we hold our breath,
As time unveils the threads of death.
Yet in this darkness, light appears,
To stitch the gaps of ancient fears.

With every heartbeat drumming near,
The echoes call, we must not fear.
For in this pulse, our fate resides,
A tapestry where hope abides.

Fables in the Cavern Embrace

In caverns deep, where shadows play,
The fables spin, their threads of gray.
With whispers soft, they weave the air,
Of creatures hidden, beyond compare.

Each corner holds a tale untold,
Where ancient spirits, brave and bold.
They linger long, in echoes bright,
Casting spells upon the night.

Through winding paths, the stories roam,
In every stone, they find a home.
A tapestry of hope and woe,
In cavern's kiss, their secrets flow.

Embrace the dark, let fables rise,
Illuminate with starlit eyes.
For in the tales that softly hum,
A world of wonder has begun.

The Weary Heart of the Hive

Within the walls of buzzing might,
A weary heart begins the flight.
In labor's dance, the workers hum,
A tale of toil, from dusk to drum.

The honey sweet, a fleeting prize,
Yet burdens weigh beneath the skies.
On fragile wings, dreams take to air,
Through nectar fields, their wishes bare.

From every bloom, the stories drench,
In unity, their strength they quench.
But shadows creep, as twilight falls,
In silence wrapped, the hive then calls.

From every sting, a lesson learned,
In bitter tears, the passion burned.
Yet still they strive, through dusk and dawn,
To find the light, to carry on.

Breathless Whispers from the Depths

Beneath the waves, the secrets sigh,
In breathless whispers, time slips by.
With every swell, a tale reborn,
Of shadows deep, where dreams are worn.

In seafoam's kiss, the echoes gleam,
A tide of thoughts, a siren's dream.
With every splash, a story sways,
In watery realms of endless days.

From coral caves, to trenches dark,
The whispers rise, igniting spark.
In currents swift, the histories weave,
Of lost souls yearning to believe.

Yet as they reach, the depths recoil,
In silent depths, their truths coiled.
Yet still they call, in watery flight,
Breathless secrets, hidden from sight.

Secrets of the Fading Fire

In twilight's grasp, the embers fade,
Whispers of warmth in shadows laid.
Moonlit dreams ignite the night,
With secrets deep, beyond our sight.

Beneath the ashes, stories dwell,
Of magic past and silent spell.
Softly told by flames anew,
As night unfurls its cloak of blue.

The stars above in twinkling dance,
Hold secrets lost in time's expanse.
Each flickering spark a tale retold,
Of love and loss, of brave and bold.

And in the flicker, hearts conspire,
To chase the dreams that never tire.
For in the dark, hope's flicker glows,
Where fading fire, true magic flows.

The Hollowed Lair of Legends

Beneath the earth where shadows creep,
The hollowed lair, secrets to keep.
Where legends whisper through the stone,
Of ancient battles, power grown.

With dust of years and echoes wide,
The tales of old within reside.
Silent guardians stand their ground,
In hallowed halls where dreams are found.

Through winding paths of moonlit gray,
The echoes call, they guide the way.
To find the truth in whispered night,
In legends born from starlit light.

Though heroes rise and heroes fall,
Their stories linger, ever call.
In hollow realms where fables live,
The heart of magic, the world they give.

Glistening Echoes of Time Forgotten

In twilight's breath, the past takes flight,
Glistening echoes in the night.
Whispers sewn in silver thread,
Of worlds long lost, where dreams have fled.

Through crystal shards of moments dear,
The laughter rings, yet none can hear.
Each shimmering fragment, a spark of fate,
In time's embrace, we hesitate.

The hours dance in moonlit beams,
Resonating our deepest dreams.
With every heartbeat, stories call,
To those who seek, to see it all.

In forgotten realms where shadows play,
The echoes guide, they light the way.
To treasure found in twilight's glow,
In glistening whispers, our hearts will know.

Vestiges of Magma's Embrace

In depths of earth where fire sleeps,
The magma breathes, its secret keeps.
Visions swirl in molten streams,
A dance of nightmares, a shower of dreams.

Within the core, the heartbeat pounds,
In fiery veins, the echo sounds.
The world above spins unaware,
Of hidden truths that lie and stare.

From ash and rock, new shapes arise,
In embers' glow, the past implies.
Each flicker holds a story's thread,
A tapestry of life once led.

With every tremor, spirits quake,
In magma's hold, the earth will wake.
For in the heat, our dreams ignite,
In vestiges of eternal night.

The Heartbeat of the Lost

In shadows deep where whispers dwell,
A tale of sorrow, few can tell.
With every beat, the silence grows,
The heart of those whom no one knows.

They wander paths of fading light,
In search of warmth, of love's delight.
Yet specters linger, haunting dreams,
And hope escapes in silent screams.

A beacon calls from far away,
But night conceals the break of day.
With every pulse, a memory fades,
In twilight's grasp, a life parades.

Through echoes lost, they roam the earth,
In the embrace of ghostly mirth.
Yet still, the heart beats strong and true,
For even lost can find what's due.

So listen close, where shadows play,
To stories spun in disarray.
For every heart that beats alone,
Holds fragments of a love unknown.

Fragmented Tales of Brimstone

In ashes cold and flames that glow,
Tales of the past begin to flow.
Each whisper burns, a tale untold,
Of courage lost and dreams of gold.

With fractured hearts, they brave the night,
Chasing shadows, seeking light.
In corners dark, the embers dance,
A fleeting chance, a fated glance.

Beneath the wrath of heaven's ire,
They weave their dreams through vile mire.
Each page a spark, each breath a fight,
To rise anew, to claim the light.

Yet in this realm of whispered sins,
The lull of dusk, the song begins.
For every scar that mars the skin,
Holds remnants of where hope has been.

So gather 'round, dear souls who roam,
To share the tales that bring us home.
For through the pain and twisted fate,
We find our bonds that cannot break.

The Lair's Lingering Song

In crumbling halls and stolen breath,
Where shadows dance with thoughts of death.
A song resounds in muted tones,
Of ancient creatures, forgotten bones.

With secrets held in every wall,
The echoes rise, the softest call.
In twilight's grasp, the whispers weave,
A tale of love that none believe.

The lair and moon entwine their grace,
In shifting light, a shadowed face.
Each note, a thread, brings forth the past,
As time slips by, too strange, too fast.

Yet in this gloom, a flicker shines,
A heartbeat lost in tangled lines.
As stories merge, entwined as one,
They dance beneath the weight of sun.

So linger here, embrace the night,
For in this place, all wrong feels right.
The song will play, a tale to share,
In whispered tones, love fills the air.

Phantoms of the Luminous Past

Beyond the veil where lost hopes sigh,
The phantoms roam, the stars awry.
In memories wrapped, they twist and turn,
With secrets kept, and hearts that yearn.

For every shadow holds a spark,
Of vibrant life that once left mark.
With every step, a ghostly glance,
A fleeting wisp, a timeless dance.

Among the ruins where echoes dwell,
The tales of triumph, love, and hell.
They linger on, these fleeting shades,
In whispered winds, the truth cascades.

Yet hope ignites through starry skies,
For in the dark, the spirit flies.
A journey paved with joy and pain,
In every heartbeat, a sweet refrain.

So cast your gaze to horizons bright,
And seek the phantoms in the light.
For every past that's left to roam,
Holds pieces of our hearts, our home.

The Last Gleam of Dusk

As twilight drapes the sky in folds,
The whispered secrets, dusk enfolds.
In shadows where the fairies dance,
Hope glimmers bright, a fleeting chance.

The stars emerge, their twinkle bold,
In myriad stories yet untold.
Beneath the boughs, the owls take flight,
Guardians of the encroaching night.

Each breath of wind, a ghostly breath,
Lurking 'neath the veil of death.
The last gleam fades, a gentle sigh,
As daybreak beckons, nigh to fly.

With hues of amber, gold, and blue,
The dawn arrives, a world anew.
Yet in the dusk, the magic stays,
In hearts so warm, and starlit ways.

Chronicles Beneath the Winged Guardian

Under the watch of a feathered sage,
Ancient tales turn a vibrant page.
Winds murmur secrets, soft as lace,
While shadows waltz, a slow embrace.

The moonlight bathes the lands in dreams,
Flowing like water, in silver streams.
Across the valleys, mist caresses,
While laughter rings, the night confesses.

In the heart of woods where stories reside,
The winged guardian, by our side.
With every flap, a history weaves,
In whispered hopes, the heart believes.

As dawn creeps in with fiery hue,
The chronicles whisper, ever true.
Beneath its wings, we chase the light,
In tales that linger within the night.

Veiled in Enigmatic Gleam

In twilight's glow, a shimmer stark,
A dance of shadows, the tendrils mark.
Through secret paths where starlight gleams,
A riddle waits beneath the dreams.

The night unfolds, a tapestry,
Woven in sighs, a mystery.
Silent whispers in the air,
Veiled in elegance, beyond compare.

Each twinkling star, a sentinel bright,
Guarding the secrets held by night.
In their embrace, lost hopes revive,
Where hearts believe and souls contrive.

Time bends softly, in a quiet dance,
As moment meets its fleeting chance.
Veiled in enigmatic gleam,
We wander through the silken dream.

Remnants of the Gleeful Glare

In the garden where the sun's embrace,
Left traces of joy, a golden grace.
Laughter lingers, like whispers soft,
In every petal, dreams aloft.

The remnants shine in the evening glow,
Where memories twinkle, ebb, and flow.
Each gentle breeze a lover's sigh,
The gleeful glare says goodbye.

As shadows stretch, they lightly tread,
On paths where the light of life had spread.
With every twinkle, joys entwine,
In every heartbeat, memories shine.

Though night may steal the radiant hour,
Each gleeful glare remains a flower.
In dormant dreams, they wait to flare,
In silence, still, we'll always care.

The Forgotten Shade's Lullaby

In shadows soft where whispers fade,
A lullaby the night had made.
The stars above in silence twink,
While dreams take flight on moonlit brink.

Dancing leaves in gentle sway,
Hold secrets of the past at bay.
A forgotten shade, with soft embrace,
Cradles the night in velvet grace.

Where echoes of the lost reside,
In twilight's hush, they gently bide.
A tale of love, now faintly sung,
In hush of night, the heartstrings strung.

Upon the breeze, the memories thread,
Of laughter shared and words unsaid.
The lullaby of time's own song,
Carries the heart where it belongs.

So close your eyes, my dear, my light,
Let dreams enfold you, hold you tight.
For in the dark, the shades will play,
A whispered night, the feared, the fey.

Mementos of Wistful Whispers

In corners deep where shadows dwell,
Mementos sit with tales to tell.
A whisper's trace, a lingering sigh,
Of moments lost as time drifts by.

The old oak chair with scuffed old frame,
Holds secrets dear, but none to name.
A dusty book that's worn and torn,
Bears stories of the dreams reborn.

Each trinket shines with wistful light,
A token of a past so bright.
Yet time must take its gentle toll,
As memories weave and softly roll.

In sheltered nooks, the heartache grows,
Yet joy persists where stillness flows.
For every whisper, every glance,
Holds a piece of love's own dance.

So gather close, the past embrace,
In mementos, find a sacred space.
For wistful whispers guide the way,
Through shadows cast in light of day.

The Crypt of Dwindled Light

Beneath the ground where time stands still,
Lies whispered dark, a ghostly thrill.
In crypts of light that softly wane,
Forgotten hopes, a lingering pain.

The flicker of a candle's glow,
Illuminates the truths we know.
In silence deep, the shadows creep,
To guard the dreams we dared to keep.

Voices echo from long ago,
A melody of loss and woe.
Yet within this somber grace,
Lies an ember's warm embrace.

For every sorrow, every tear,
Has crafted tales for us to hear.
In crypt so deep, the light may fade,
But love's remembrance will not trade.

So seek the light within the shade,
And let the past's own charm cascade.
For in the dark, a truth will bloom,
Lighting the path to lift the gloom.

Agates Beneath the Scorched Sky

Across the land where shadows play,
Agates gleam in the light of day.
Beneath the scorched and blazing sun,
A tale of resilience has begun.

Each stone a heart in colors bright,
Hold echoes of the long-lost fight.
They whisper strength against the heat,
In every crack, a story's seat.

The desert winds, they weave and swirl,
As sand and stone in chaos twirl.
Yet in the midst of stark despair,
A beauty blooms, beyond compare.

Through trials faced beneath this dome,
The agates shine, they call us home.
For in each facet, wisdom's grace,
Reminds us all of our own place.

So walk the path where stones align,
And find the light in each design.
For agates 'neath the scorched sky's eye,
Carry the dreams of those who try.

Shadows Playing in the Dragon's Den

In the caverns deep where whispers dwell,
Silhouettes of secrets cast their spell.
Flickering flames in the colder gloom,
Echoes of laughter in the dragon's room.

Beneath the scales of emerald green,
Shadows dance where no one's seen.
Rustling wings in the distance sway,
Guarding stories from the light of day.

Treasures piled in haphazard heaps,
A realm where time itself just sleeps.
In the hush of the night, a flicker flies,
The beating heart of ancient skies.

Crackling fires forge an omen bold,
While tales of yore whisper stories told.
Yet in the depths, the past shall reign,
In shadows playing, joy and pain.

In the dragon's realm, where dusk takes flight,
Night unveils the boldest sight.
So step lightly where legends tread,
In the dragon's den, where none dare head.

Glinting Treasures of the Wyrm's Keep

In the vaults where glittering gems reside,
The wyrm's keep that none can guide.
Starlight captured in facets bright,
Guarded fiercely from the night.

Echoes whisper of fortunes grand,
Riches nestled in ancient sand.
A hoard of dreams in a jeweled chest,
Waiting for hearts that dare to quest.

Through vaulted halls where shadows creep,
Lies the promise of secrets deep.
Treasures of silver, gold, and stone,
In the dark where the wyrm has grown.

In hidden nooks and crannies wide,
Glinting treasures seem to bide.
Each spark a wish, a tale untold,
A siren's song in the dark and cold.

Beyond the guard of fiery breath,
Awaits a chance to cheat the death.
Yet many seek and many fall,
To claim the wyrm's treasure, who shall call?

The Faded Echo of Serpent Dreams

Amidst the whispers of the twilight veil,
Lie the remnants of a forgotten tale.
Serpents curling in shadows deep,
Where echoes of dreams have lost their keep.

Woven paths of glittering thread,
Mark the journey of the once revered.
Faded visions in silver light,
Cradle the histories of the night.

Beneath the moon's soft, ghostly glow,
Serpents stir in the silent flow.
Dreams of glory, now whispers frail,
Echo through time like a distant wail.

In the silence where magic swells,
Rest the stories the serpent tells.
Of valor and caution, love and dread,
A haunting refrain where all have fled.

Yet through the shadows, hope will creep,
For even faded dreams may leap.
To kindle the fire of past reborn,
In the echoes of night, a new day's dawn.

Secrets of the Scorched Orchard

In the orchard where shadows burn,
Secrets linger for those who yearn.
Trees once green now whisper low,
Of treasures lost in an ember glow.

Branches twisted in the searing heat,
Tell of tales where hearts may meet.
Ripened dreams, a bittersweet taste,
In the shadows, not a moment to waste.

Beneath the ash of forgotten lore,
Lie fruits of magic, forevermore.
Sweetness tainted by the flames below,
In the orchard where true secrets flow.

Burgeoning roots that ache with woe,
Cradle the cries of a world forebode.
Insolent winds weave a somber song,
And in this place, nothing feels wrong.

Yet hope may grow where fire had cursed,
For life finds a way through shadows rehearsed.
From the scorched earth, a new dawn will break,
In the secrets of the orchard, hearts will wake.

Sirens of the Breached Vault

In the depths where silence sways,
Echoes weave through the darkened maze.
Voices call with sweet allure,
Luring souls to depths unsure.

Glimmers fade, hope starts to wane,
Chasing whispers of joy and pain.
Through crackling air, the secrets glide,
In the shadows where fears reside.

Lights flicker in grim embrace,
Shadows dance in a timeless space.
Yet the sirens' song won't last,
As echoes fade into the past.

Beyond the vault, what lies ahead?
Unraveled paths where dreams have bled.
Only those who dare will see,
The secrets held in destiny.

Hear the call that bends the light,
Into the depths of endless night.
Sirens sing their haunting tune,
While the stars fade beneath the moon.

Shadows Beneath the Wing

Beneath the spread of twilight's cloak,
Whispers stir as dreams provoke.
Feathers brush against soft air,
Casting shadows unaware.

In the fold where secrets lie,
Mysteries in a silent sigh.
Winged creatures glide with grace,
In the darkness, they embrace.

Winds of fortune, tales untold,
Stories shimmer, shy yet bold.
Guided by the moon's soft glow,
Revealing paths we long to know.

Lurking figures, soft and sly,
Among the branches, spirits fly.
A tapestry of night unfurls,
In every shadow, magic twirls.

Seek the truth in feathered flight,
Hidden worlds in the softest night.
For shadows dance with ancient song,
In the tales that linger long.

The Faded Resplendence

Once in glory, bright and bold,
Wiser tales of years retold.
Echoes whisper through the veil,
Haunting dreams of light grown pale.

With every glance, the past remains,
Wrapped in threads of golden chains.
Faded hues on weathered stones,
Trace the memories of old thrones.

In gardens where the shadows bloom,
Lies a sense of fading doom.
Yet amongst the withered grace,
Hope resides in a secret place.

Lingering scents of blooming night,
Recall the days of pure delight.
Yet time flows like a gentle stream,
Carrying forth a tepid dream.

Resplendence lost, yet not in vain,
Life cycles through joy and pain.
In the heart where dreams combine,
Faded glories intertwine.

Chimeras in the Flickering Gloom

In the corners where shadows play,
Chimeras laugh and twist away.
Flickering flames, uncertain light,
Mask the truths that haunt the night.

Figures dart in a ghostly dance,
A veil of time and circumstance.
Ogres brave and sprites so small,
Weaving spells through the twilight's call.

Lost in dreams, the heart must fight,
To pierce the veil of endless night.
For every fear, a courage blooms,
Amidst the chimeras in the gloom.

Echoes murmur through twisted trees,
As voices rise on the evening breeze.
Illusions drift like wispy smoke,
In the depths where shadows cloak.

Yet through the haze, hope's beacon shines,
Illuminating the tangled lines.
For when the dawn begins to loom,
Chimeras fade, dispelled by bloom.

Worn Wonders in the Hidden Keep

In shadows deep, where secrets nest,
The keep holds stories, never confessed.
Worn wonders whisper of battles fought,
Echoes of magic, into silence caught.

Ancient tapestries cling to the walls,
With tales of glory, as mystery calls.
Each thread a moment, a heart that yearned,
For lost adventures, forever burned.

The lanterns flicker, casting soft light,
On armor rusted from the endless night.
Dreams of the brave that once stood tall,
Now curled like leaves, destined to fall.

In corners cobwebbed, they lie in wait,
Curiosities wrapped in the hands of fate.
A tapestry unfurling, revealing the past,
Of heroes and shadows, forever cast.

With every creak of the hallowed floor,
Legends arise, and then fade once more.
The hidden keep keeps its secrets still,
Worn wonders linger, tempered by will.

Secrets of the Scaled Sanctuary

In the heart of the woods, where silence sings,
Lies a sanctuary, where magic clings.
Scaled creatures slumber beneath ancient trees,
Guarding their secrets, their mysteries tease.

The air thick with whispers, a promise behold,
Of stories long lost, of treasures untold.
Each scale that glimmers in dappled light,
Holds the essence of dreams taking flight.

Within leafy boughs, shadows abound,
Where flickering eyes watch without a sound.
Innocence trembles, as the night grows deep,
For secrets awaken, from their timeless sleep.

The moon paints their scales with a shimmering hue,
Casting spells of enchantment, the old and the new.
For every brave heart that dares to explore,
The sanctuary keeps, forevermore.

A treasure of truth in the still of the night,
Where secrets of scales blend with the light.
In the shifting shadows, a journey begins,
To uncover the magic where wonder wins.

The Lament of the Lost Jewel

Once a jewel, shining bright as the dawn,
Now a whisper of light, forever withdrawn.
It gleamed with stories of love and despair,
A treasure forgotten, a heart laid bare.

In the echoes of time, its voice still calls,
Through sapphire skies and ancient halls.
Each lament it weaves in the fabric of night,
Holds the weight of wishes, lost in flight.

Cradled in shadows, its brilliance fades,
A memory trapped where the ambers cascade.
To find what was lost, a quest now unfolds,
In the land of the brave, where the truth beholds.

Casting reflections in glimmers of gold,
The jewel remembers the tales it told.
Within every tear lies a history spun,
Of battles and triumphs, all lost but one.

The world grows tired, but the jewel remains,
In the heart of the night, where longing reigns.
Its lament echoes softly, a haunting refrain,
For the love that was lost, and the dreams that remain.

Dusty Relics of a Fiery Realm

In the depths of a realm where the embers glow,
Dusty relics whisper of long-ago.
Once they blazed bright, a testament true,
Now resting in silence, a somber hue.

Scorched earth and shadows, they tell of the age,
Of fiery beasts, and a war's bitter rage.
Fragments of memories cling to the dust,
In their stories reside the echoes of trust.

The air is thick with the scent of despair,
As each relic yearns for a soul to care.
Honor their past, honor their plight,
In the silence of ashes, they hold onto light.

Old banners fray in the warm, gentle breeze,
Each thread a story of victories seized.
Ancient crystals, once bright with flame,
Now lie in slumber, forgotten their name.

Yet from the dusk rise new dreams to ignite,
With courage and faith, they embrace the night.
Dusty relics linger, their spirits still strong,
Waiting for hearts that will right the wrong.

Treasures Lost in Ember's Dream

In the whispering winds where shadows play,
The treasures of night begin to sway.
Flickering flames of forgotten lore,
Awaiting the brave to unlock the door.

Through realms unseen, where phantoms tread,
Lies a heart once bright, now veiled in dread.
Ember's glow casts tales of old,
Beneath the stars, their secrets unfold.

Adventurers come with eyes alight,
Chasing the echoes of endless night.
Yet amidst the gems, a riddle lies,
Glimmers of truth within the lies.

Past the thickets, where wild dreams soar,
Find the whispering voices of yore.
For in the silence, the treasures gleam,
Waiting for those who dare to dream.

With each step closer, the shadows weave,
A tapestry rich, of loss and reprieve.
The path is perilous, the choices stark,
In ember's embrace, ignite the spark.

Dusty Echoes of the Dragon's Grief

Amidst the ruins where dragons weep,
Old tales linger, their secrets deep.
Dusty echoes dance on the breeze,
Whispers of sorrow beneath the trees.

Once mighty wings now frail and torn,
A guardian's heart, weary and worn.
Through empty halls, its memories sigh,
In the twilight glow of a fading sky.

The treasures amassed in scales of gold,
Echo the pain of stories untold.
Each glint of light, a fragment stark,
Flickers of life in the cold and dark.

In caverns vast, through shadows wide,
Linger the spirits that once defied.
From ashes they rise, a haunting refrain,
Of loss, love, and enduring pain.

Yet in this grief, a spark remains,
A flicker of hope despite the chains.
For every end whispers sweet release,
In dusty echoes, may dragons find peace.

The Silent Watcher in the Caverns

In the depth of night, where secrets dream,
A silent watcher keeps the gleam.
Hidden in shadows, no eyes can see,
Guarding the silence, patient and free.

Ancient stones echo the tales of old,
Of battles fought and treasures bold.
Chilling whispers beckon from the deep,
While time itself dares not to sleep.

Each heartbeat echoes, a rhythmic sigh,
Beneath the earth where the lost souls lie.
Guided by starlight, a soft embrace,
In the labyrinth, they find their place.

Caverns unfold like a tale unwritten,
Beneath the weight of all that's smitten.
The watcher listens, with wisdom grand,
Holding the dreams of a forgotten land.

Through silken darkness, the truth will bloom,
In silence profound, dispelling the gloom.
For in the stillness, a voice will rise,
The silent watcher, a bridge to the skies.

Ghosts of a Glimmering Past

In the twilight glow, where shadows blend,
Dance the ghosts of time, our age-old friends.
Flickering memories, soft and bright,
Whispering stories in the sapphire night.

Echoes of laughter, hearts entwined,
Tales of the brave, the lost, the kind.
Past glimmers shine with a radiant light,
Entwined in the fabric of day and night.

Through the mist, where secrets weave,
Ghosts linger softly, urging us to believe.
In every shimmer, a promise lies,
As they guide us toward the endless skies.

With every step on this path we tread,
The shadows of yore nourish the thread.
For in the past flows our present's song,
Ghosts remind us where we belong.

So cherish the moments, both near and far,
In the tapestry spun beneath each star.
For ghostly whispers and glimmers cast,
Are reminders of love in a glimmering past.

The Essence of Forgotten Light

In shadows cast by ancient trees,
Whispers wind with gentle ease.
A beacon lost to time's embrace,
Flickers softly in this place.

Echoes of the day grown dim,
Dance upon a twilight brim.
Memories like fireflies twirl,
In the heart of twilight's whirl.

Secrets held in amber hue,
Each moment tinged with golden dew.
From the depths, a soft refrain,
Calls the spirit back again.

Rays of hope through branches weave,
Promising what we believe.
A destiny entwined with night,
Awaits in the forgotten light.

Cryptic Stories of Scorched Dreams

In the ashes lies a tale,
Of spirits lost and winds that wail.
A canvas marred by sorrow's hand,
Paints the dreams that never spanned.

Flickering shadows on the ground,
Whispers of hope that soon drowned.
Silent screams in the burning air,
Echoes of what once was fair.

Beneath the charred and weary sky,
One must search for reasons why.
Fragments of the past entwined,
In the heart, the lost are blind.

A journey through the haunting flames,
Reveals the world without its names.
For every dream that turns to dust,
Lies the power of rebirth's trust.

Enigmas of the Serpentine Keep

Within the walls of stone so old,
Lies a tapestry of secrets untold.
Winding paths with whispers steep,
Guard the lore the shadows keep.

Twists and turns in lantern light,
Guide the brave through endless night.
As cobwebs cling in eerie calm,
Unfolding tales, their quiet charm.

A serpent's gaze through ages peered,
Every wish and dream declared.
In the heart of silence dwells
A magic where the darkness swells.

Forgotten prophecies entwined,
With the hearts of those confined.
In each chamber, every seam,
Whispers thread a silver dream.

The Glimmering Dust in Twilight

As twilight tints the sky with grace,
Glimmering dust begins to trace.
A mist of dreams clings overhead,
Leading hearts where they are led.

Across the fields where shadows meet,
The softest whispers, secrets sweet.
Each twinkle sparkles, bids adieu,
To everything we thought we knew.

In the stillness, wishes bloom,
Twilight's brush erases gloom.
Time weaves through the cosmic air,
Gifting whispers, gentle flare.

A dance of stars ignites the night,
Chasing echoes of lost light.
In glimmering dust, we find our way,
To a brighter dawn from yesterday.

Soot-Stained Secrets of the Ember Nest

In shadows deep where embers glow,
Whispers dance on the winds that blow.
Secrets hide in the ash and light,
Soot-stained tales of the long, dark night.

Nestled high where the blazes flare,
Fables linger in the smoky air.
Fragments of dreams in the flicker caught,
Lessons learned in the fire's thought.

A phoenix sings of its restless flight,
Crafted from pain, reborn in spite.
Each tear a gem, each scar a mark,
Transforming the tales from light to dark.

Among the cinders fortune gleams,
Echoing softly in distant dreams.
With ashes buried, the truth takes wing,
Soot-stained secrets that embers bring.

So heed the whispers, let shadows guide,
In the nest of flames, let your heart confide.
For in the darkness, the light is prized,
In soot-stained secrets, the soul is sized.

Whispered Tales Beneath the Scales

In caverns deep where shadows creep,
The serpent stirs from its ancient sleep.
Beneath the scales, stories twine,
Whispered echoes of the divine.

Wisdom wrapped in a silken coil,
Secrets buried in the soil.
Fables woven with care and grace,
In the flicker of light, find your place.

From the depths, the echoes arise,
Dreams entwined with the stars in the skies.
Each tale a thread, each thread a life,
Woven through joy, through sorrow, and strife.

Listen closer, let the stories flow,
In the realm of the hidden, the heart can grow.
For beneath each scale, a truth awaits,
A whispered tale of the fates and mates.

So venture forth where the shadows dwell,
In the serpent's song, weave your spell.
For in the murmur of twilight's grace,
Lie whispered tales beneath each scale.

Ashen Fruits of the Mystic Grove

In the grove where the shadows blend,
Beneath the boughs where the night winds wend.
Fruits hang low with a smoky hue,
Whispers sweet in the twilight dew.

Each ashen fruit tells a tale unknown,
Of dreams once lost and seeds once sown.
Beneath the bark, the stories sing,
Of fire and feathers, the dance of spring.

In the stillness, a soft wind sighs,
A gentle hush as the darkness flies.
With twilight's touch, the magic swells,
In each ashen fruit, a secret dwells.

To taste the truth, you must be brave,
For in its sweetness, the heart can save.
Reach out and pluck, let your spirit soar,
For the mystic grove holds so much more.

So wander forth and let it be,
The ashen fruits shall set you free.
In the heart of the grove, let the magic glove,
Reveal the secrets of your heart's love.

Glimmers Lost in the Lair of Fire

In the lair where the flames do dance,
Glimmers lost in a fiery trance.
Flickering shadows upon the stone,
Tales of valor in whispers grown.

Amidst the heat, a treasure sleeps,
Secrets buried in the silence keeps.
Each spark a memory, faint yet bright,
In the heart of darkness, a flicker of light.

From embered depths, a voice calls clear,
Finding warmth in the shadows near.
Courage kindles where fear once lay,
Glimmers lost now lead the way.

So delve into the warmth and heat,
Where glimmers dance and shadows meet.
With every flicker, let your heart aspire,
To find your truth in the lair of fire.

For in that place where the light is shy,
Lie glimmers lost that never die.
Seek the warmth, let hope inspire,
In the depths and dreams of the lair of fire.

Echoing Dreams of the Serpent's Cave

In shadows deep where whispers cling,
The serpent coiled, a dreamer's king.
Beneath the stones, the echoes play,
Of moonlit nights, of dusk till day.

With every hiss, a tale unfolds,
Of treasures lost, and secrets told.
The cave, a womb of darkened fears,
Where hope and despair dance with tears.

Through winding paths of ancient stone,
The heart of dreams remains alone.
Yet glimmers shine in darkest depths,
A promise kept, a world adept.

So wander not with empty hearts,
For in the dark, the magic starts.
Embrace the dreams of serpent's fate,
Unlock the doors that fate creates.

The winds will carry soft the song,
Of life and loss, where we belong.
So heed the call, let shadows weave,
The serpent's cave, where we believe.

Fragments of a Shattered Myths

Once bold and bright, the stories soared,
Now fragments lie where dreams were stored.
Old legends whisper through the trees,
As fleeting thoughts caught in the breeze.

Noble knights and dragons fair,
Now cobwebs cling to dreams laid bare.
From dawn to dusk, they often fade,
Yet still, the heart is unafraid.

Each broken shard a tale to tell,
Of love and loss, of heaven and hell.
In twilight's embrace, they softly call,
To those who dare to heed their thrall.

Though myths may shatter, hearts won't yield,
For in each fragment, hope is sealed.
Let memories flow like rivers wide,
In shattered tales, our dreams abide.

With every piece, a spark of light,
Guiding lost souls through darkest night.
Embrace the shards, the story's grace,
For shattered myths have their own place.

The Dragon's Diminished Hoard

In caverns deep, where shadows creep,
The mighty dragon guards its keep.
But treasures lost to time's cruel hand,
Lay scattered wide across the land.

Once glittering jewels and gleaming gold,
Now whispers of tales long retold.
The fire within, once fierce and bright,
Now flickers low, despite the night.

The dragon sighs for days of yore,
When hoards were rich, and dreams could soar.
A heart of flame, now dimmed to gray,
Yet still, it watches, night and day.

In quiet moments, hope remains,
That past glories may break the chains.
For even in loss, beauty blooms,
In dragon's dreams, the magic looms.

So tread with care, and hold them near,
The tales of old, once loud and clear.
For in the heart of every beast,
Lies a treasure that will never cease.

Silhouettes in the Crystal Grotto

In the grotto where crystal shines,
Silhouettes dance in twisted lines.
Reflections flicker, soft and bright,
Whispers echo through the night.

Each stalactite, a memory caught,
Of dreams pursued, of lessons taught.
In glittering walls, secrets weave,
A tapestry of hope to believe.

Glimmers of past in every hue,
Invite the wanderer to pursue.
Through winding paths, where shadows fade,
A journey new, where truth is laid.

With every step, the heart may change,
Embracing paths both wide and strange.
In crystal light, the soul does soar,
Discovering worlds, forevermore.

So linger long where dreams reside,
In the grotto's embrace, let life abide.
For silhouettes that softly glow,
Guide the lost to future's flow.

Remains of the Spirited Glow

In the shadows where whispers tread,
A shimmer glows, though hope seems dead.
The laughter echoes, soft and low,
Remnants linger of a vibrant show.

Beneath the stars that flicker bright,
Dreams once soared, now take flight.
With every breath, the memories rise,
Embers dance beneath the skies.

Silent secrets fill the air,
Caught in twilight, caught in care.
The past draws near, a glowing thread,
Binding hearts where dreams have bled.

From crumbling walls of ancient stone,
The spirit whispers, never alone.
Through tangled paths and flickered flame,
We find the spark, we speak its name.

So let us walk through shadowed halls,
Where every echo faintly calls.
The spirited glow will always flow,
In hearts that dare to dream and grow.

Chronicles from the Gloomy Depths

In caverns dark, where shadows creep,
Lies the silence, cluttered, deep.
Tales unfurl in dim-lit gloom,
With secrets sealed in endless tomb.

Ghostly figures swirl and weave,
In whispers soft, they dare believe.
Each murmur tells of ages past,
Where time itself became an outcast.

Beneath the weight of ancient stone,
Chronicles of sorrow moan.
Every crevice, every sigh,
Reflects the dreams that dared to die.

A glimmer shines, an ember's spark,
A fragile hope in silence stark.
With courage found in shadows' clutch,
The stories rise, they long for touch.

So venture forth to hear their plea,
For in the depths, the sea runs free.
Through every tale, shadows blend,
The past and present twists, transcends.

The Flicker of an Ancient Flame

In the heart of night, a whisper glows,
An ancient flame that softly flows.
With every flicker, tales unfold,
Of journeys bright, and legends old.

Through veils of time, it weaves a thread,
Connecting lives, both lost and led.
A dance of shadows, a spark of light,
In every breath, it banishes night.

When darkness falls and silence reigns,
The flame persists through all the pains.
With every pulse, a heartbeat true,
It chants the wisdom, old and new.

And though the winds may rise and roar,
The ancient flame stands evermore.
It flickers still in hearts that dare,
To chase the light, to seek and share.

So gather round and heed the song,
Of the ancient flame, both proud and strong.
For in its light, our spirits soar,
A flicker whispering forevermore.

Crystallized Myths at Twilight

As daylight fades and shadows sing,
Crystallized myths take gentle wing.
In twilight's grasp, the stories shine,
Each fragment glimmers, intertwine.

From forgotten realms, they drift and play,
Echoes of dreams that slipped away.
With every star that starts to gleam,
The legends flood, the spirits teem.

In shimmering hues of violet hue,
Whispers awaken, ancient and true.
Their voices weave a timeless dance,
Entwined in fate, we take a chance.

With hearts aflame beneath the skies,
We chase the myths, where wonder lies.
Through crystal tears and laughter bright,
We bind the stories in the night.

So linger here, where dreams ignite,
Crystallized myths, a pure delight.
In twilight's arms, let the magic flow,
For in its glow, our spirits grow.

Cinders of Longing in the Hollowed Stone

In the quiet dusk, dreams softly weep,
Echoes of vows that secrets keep.
Amidst the shadows, hearts entwined,
Yearning whispers in the wind confined.

A moonlit glimmer on ancient walls,
Where hope lingers and despair calls.
Fragments of laughter, now faded sighs,
Beneath the stars, where time slowly flies.

Beneath the stone, embers glow bright,
Flickering souls in the still of night.
In cinders of longing, a truth remains,
Passion unfurls, yet sorrow reigns.

In the hollowed hearts, love's ember burns,
With every moment, the tide still turns.
Through misty veils, the past takes flight,
In shadows of hope, we chase the light.

Shattered Lights in the Wyrm's Wake

In the dragon's roar, a tale untold,
Brave souls have ventured, and legends bold.
With eyes aflame and wings spread wide,
They dance with fate in the moonlight's tide.

Amidst the ruins where shadows creep,
Fragments of dreams lie lost and deep.
Crimson stars fall from skies of ash,
And in their descent, the memories clash.

The wyrm's fierce heart, both cruel and wise,
Gazes upon the fallen skies.
With shattered lights, the hopes entwine,
In every crack, a story divine.

Through ancient verses, the truth ignites,
Finding solace in the still of nights.
Where dragons wail and the lost still pray,
In shattered lights, we find our way.

Frayed Whispers from the Fiery Abyss

In the depths where shadows sing,
Frayed whispers dance on the edge of spring.
With fiery breath that burns the cold,
Stories of courage in silence unfold.

The chasm calls with a voice like thunder,
Lured by secrets too deep to plunder.
Crimson tendrils weave through the dark,
Each flicker a promise, each spark a mark.

In the abyss where lost souls roam,
Echos of longing find their home.
Courage ignites with every tear,
As hope rekindles, drawing near.

Through fiery trials, hearts become pure,
In whispers frayed, we learn to endure.
Bound by the ashes of dreams once bold,
Our stories of grace in the embers told.

Eclipsed Glories of the Dragon's Cradle

In the cradle of stars, where shadows blend,
Eclipsed glories whisper, hearts to mend.
With dragon's flight in twilight's embrace,
We seek the warmth of a forgotten place.

Once bright dreams dimmed in time's great waltz,
Yet hope lingers, despite life's faults.
Mirrored in tears, the past remains,
While echoes of laughter break our chains.

Here legends sleep beneath ancient trees,
Cradled in secrets carried by the breeze.
Through twilight's veil, a promise unfurls,
In the dragon's cradle, our fate twirls.

In eclipsed glories, the heart takes flight,
With every shadow, we chase the light.
Bound by the echoes of dreams once grand,
Together we rise, hand in hand.

Varnished Hues of the Slumbering Flame

In twilight's grasp, the embers glow,
Whispers dance in the warm winds' flow.
Colors flicker from deep within,
A story waiting for hearts to spin.

Shadows play on the wall of night,
Crimson blush mingles with golden light.
Each hue a tale of joy and woe,
Nestled close where the secrets grow.

From ashes rise, the dreams reborn,
A phoenix cries as the stars are worn.
Varnished tales of the fire's art,
Binding the night to the yearning heart.

Echoes linger in the still of air,
Weight of moments lost in despair.
Yet among them, a promise gleams,
In every flicker, there dance the dreams.

So take a breath, let the warmth embrace,
Feel the rhythm of the flames' soft grace.
For in each spark lies a timeless claim,
In varnished hues, we find our name.

Dusty Echoes of Forgotten Legends

In tomes long closed, the whispers dwell,
Tales of heroes, their rise and fell.
Dusty echoes in chambers lost,
Yesterday's glories, a heavy cost.

The wind carries songs of long ago,
In ancient ruins, the shadows grow.
Forgotten paths where the brave once trod,
Buried deep in the myths of the sod.

Each cracked page holds a truth untold,
A flicker of warmth in the bitter cold.
Legends linger like a shadowed sigh,
Waiting for hearts who dare to try.

In every tale, a lesson we find,
A thread that weaves through all mankind.
Dare to revive the dreams long past,
In dusty echoes, our hopes are cast.

So lift the veil and breathe in the lore,
For in our stories, we live once more.
In the tapestry of time, we see
The dusty echoes that set us free.

Charred Blossoms in the Heart of the Mountain

Where the peaks rise to kiss the sky,
Life blooms bright where the shadows lie.
Among the stones and the ash-streaked earth,
Charred blossoms whisper of rebirth.

In craggy cliffs, the wildflowers sway,
Defying the fire that lead them astray.
Their colors vibrant against the grey,
A testament to the last display.

From smoldering roots, new life ignites,
In the heart of darkness, the soul delights.
Each petal tells of the journey's strain,
In every bruise, there blooms a gain.

Through trials faced in the mountain's breath,
We rise anew from the ashes of death.
Charred blossoms blossom under the moon,
Singing sweet songs of an ancient tune.

So stand in awe, let your spirit soar,
For in the struggle, we find what's more.
In charred blossoms, the heart can see,
The beauty of life in our destiny.

Resplendent Echoes of the Hidden Vault

In chambers deep, where shadows creep,
Resplendent echoes gently sweep.
Secrets tucked in the folds of time,
Guarded treasures, oh so sublime.

The heart beats softly as whispers slide,
Through golden keys where the memories hide.
Unlocking doors with each gentle touch,
In the hidden vault, we crave so much.

With every breath, the past awakes,
In raptured silence, my spirit shakes.
Lost souls dance in a swirling dream,
In echo chambers, we hear their scheme.

Oh, what wonders in darkness dwell,
A story woven with a glimmering spell.
Resplendent echoes of love and strife,
Lingering softly, they sing of life.

So wander deep where the shadows pause,
In forgotten corners, embrace the cause.
For in every echo, a voice will call,
In the hidden vault, we are one and all.

Relics of Ruined Realms

In shadows deep where echoes dwell,
Old kingdoms whisper, tales to tell.
Fragmented hopes in crumbling stone,
Ghosts of glory, forever alone.

The winds of time through arches sigh,
Beneath the watchful, starlit sky.
Ancient runes on weathered walls,
Forge the fate of those who fall.

Lost treasures wait in silenced halls,
Guarded by fate's relentless calls.
A tapestry of dreams entwined,
In every crease, a moment defined.

The mystic waters, still and clear,
Reflect the past, draw ever near.
A labyrinth of secrets veiled,
Where hope and truth have sometimes failed.

But in the dusk, new spirits rise,
Reclaiming shadows 'neath the skies.
For every ruin tells its tale,
A promise wrapped within the veil.

The Enigma of Lost Luminescence

In twilight's grasp, the stars fade low,
Whispers of light begin to glow.
An echo of dreams once bold and bright,
Chasing shadows through the night.

A lantern's flicker, a beacon lost,
Guiding souls at any cost.
Through tangled woods and whispers faint,
A fleeting heart, a wayward saint.

Luminescence born from sighs,
A tapestry of evening skies.
Fractured beams in silence fall,
Yet still they beckon, call us all.

In every heart, a spark remains,
A thread of hope that breaks the chains.
Though darkness veils what once was clear,
Remember, love will conquer fear.

The enigma dances in our souls,
For every void still has its goals.
Through losses deep, let courage rise,
As dawn awakens in new skies.

Song of the Withered Flame

A flicker in the ashes gray,
Whispers of warmth from yesterday.
Where embers linger, soft and low,
The song of flames begins to flow.

Tales of fire in every breath,
A fervent dance between life and death.
With every spark, a memory glows,
In ancient hearts, the fervor grows.

Yet shadows creep where fervor fades,
In silence deep, the light cascades.
A smoldering dream, pressed in the past,
Clings to the warmth that could not last.

But still we gather, hands intertwined,
To stoke the embers that fate designed.
For in our hearts, the flame can rise,
Transforming ashes to azure skies.

So let us sing, though flames are thin,
A melody born from within.
Through withered time, our spirits soar,
In every song, the fire restores.

Reflections in the Emerald Abyss

In depths profound where silence reigns,
Emerald tides wash lost refrains.
Mirrored tales in waters deep,
Secrets that the shadows keep.

Glistening depths like dreams untold,
Whisper secrets from ages old.
Luminous echoes rise and fall,
Beneath the waves, we hear the call.

The abyss hides a fleeting glance,
Of starlit wonders, a fated dance.
Through liquid veil, the past ignites,
Where memories sail on sapphire nights.

Yet in the calm, a tempest brews,
As heartbeats mimic the ocean's blues.
Each ripple holds a thousand fears,
Reflected in the traveler's tears.

But courage stirs in twilight's breath,
A journey blooms beyond the depth.
For in the abyss, we find our place,
Emerald waters, a sacred space.

Whispers of Weathered Treasures

Beneath the stormy skies so wide,
Old tales of yore begin to glide.
A silver ship with tattered sail,
Whispers secrets of a hidden trail.

The waves like fingers stroke the sand,
In twilight's grasp, a treasure planned.
With every gasp of the cool night air,
Echoes linger, a mystic dare.

The lanterns gleam with tales untold,
Where dreams of daring hearts unfold.
In shadows deep, the past awakes,
A map of fate that history makes.

Castles crumbling, ivy's embrace,
Nature's brush on time's soft face.
Each pebble holds a story keen,
In the twilight's hush, it can be seen.

Shadows Amongst the Scales

In the forest where the mermaids dwell,
A tale of scales, a whispered spell.
With glimmering eyes, they swim and sway,
In the twilight's dance, they slip away.

Like ribbons of silver around the creek,
The shadows play, they skip and peek.
Among the reeds, secrets do lie,
In the glens where the fairies sigh.

Touched by moonlight, a magical view,
The water breathes, its spirit true.
In unfamiliar depths, silence reigns,
Guarding the treasures, a love that pains.

With laughter echoing, they glide with ease,
Bound by twilight, a gentle breeze.
These creatures of dusk, elusive, rare,
In shadows deep, they breathe the air.

Echoes from the Cavern Heart

Deep in the earth, where silence reigns,
A cavern whispers of long-lost gains.
Stalactites gleam in a spectral dance,
Holding secrets of fate and chance.

Water drips in a rhythmic chant,
Each droplet sings, a shimmering grant.
In corners dark, shadows take flight,
Echoes of dreams fade into night.

Crystals jut from the stone's embrace,
A timeless heart, an ageless face.
With every step, the past draws near,
A symphony played on the strings of fear.

Footsteps echo, resonating deep,
Guarding the secrets that the shadows keep.
In this embrace of damp and chill,
Lies a mystery, a haunting thrill.

Glimmers of Forgotten Gems

In ancient woods where shadows creep,
Forgotten gems in silence sleep.
Buried deep where time stands still,
Lies the whispers of a bygone thrill.

With every breeze, a tale awakes,
In the rustling leaves, nature quakes.
Sparkling bright in the fading light,
These treasures of earth, a wondrous sight.

Once they danced in the sun's warm glow,
Now hidden paths where few may go.
Each bead of light a story spun,
In a place where the rivers run.

Beneath the roots, in soil so rich,
Lies the magic, a timeless stitch.
Glimmers beckon from rocky seams,
In the hush of dusk, the heart still dreams.

Dull Glimmers in the Heart of the Beast

In shadows deep where silence sleeps,
A pulse of pain the darkness keeps,
Beneath the scales, a flicker bright,
A spark of hope amidst the night.

With every breath, the echoes cry,
Of dreams long lost that fade and die,
Yet in the gloom, a whisper stirs,
A promise held in gentle furs.

The beast may roar, but soft the heart,
With tender notes that pull apart,
The chains of grief that bind its soul,
To find the light and make it whole.

Amidst the thorns, a glimmer glows,
A magic born from hidden throes,
In every tear, a story flows,
To heal the wounds that time bestows.

So seek the dull glimmers that gleam,
For in despair, we find a dream,
And in the heart of what we fear,
Lies strength anew, though faint and near.

Legends Veiled in the Ashen Forest

In an ashen land where shadows play,
The whispers of old legends sway,
Ghostly tales on the breath of trees,
Carried softly by the autumn breeze.

The roots entwined in secrets deep,
Guard the stories that time will keep,
Of knights and quests and dragons bold,
In echoes of glory, their fates unfold.

Through mists that curl like silver threads,
The forest sleeps where magic treads,
With every step, a memory sings,
Of ancient woods and forgotten kings.

Yet fear not the shadows that creep,
For in the dark, the brave can leap,
To find the light where legends dwell,
In the heart of the woods, a sacred spell.

Let the ashen forest remind us all,
That legends rise and legends fall,
But in each tale, a truth endures,
A spark of hope that love ensures.

Lightless Gems in the Dragon's Embrace

In caverns dark where dragons sleep,
Lie lightless gems in silence deep,
Whispers echo, ancient and low,
Guardians of secrets only they know.

With scales like night and breath of fire,
These creatures dwell in lost desire,
For every gem, a story spun,
Of battles fought and victories won.

Yet hidden hearts beneath the pain,
Yearn for warmth, a touch of rain,
In hoarded treasures, dreams reside,
Waiting for hearts to open wide.

The dragon's embrace, fierce and tight,
Hides treasures bright from mortal sight,
But love, like light, will surely find,
The path to soften what's confined.

So seek the gems in shadows cast,
For even darkness cannot last,
And in the depths, the truth will gleam,
A hope reborn, a waking dream.

Mysteries Entwined in the Serpent's Grasp

In tangled coils where secrets whisper,
A serpent waits, its gaze a glister,
With emerald scales and eyes of gold,
It knows the stories yet untold.

Beneath the moon's unyielding glare,
The mysteries swirl in twilight air,
Each riddle wrapped in silver light,
A dance of shadows, dark and bright.

In the serpent's grasp, we find the key,
To unlock the past, to set it free,
For wisdom lies in winding paths,
In every twist, the truth just bathes.

Though fear may coil around the heart,
Courage blooms in shadows' art,
To wrestle with the unknown's face,
And find the strength to embrace grace.

So let us wander through the night,
With trust that guides our seeking sight,
For in the serpent's cryptic plea,
Lies a tapestry of destiny.

Echoes in the Scaled Hollow

In the hollow where shadows dwell,
Whispers breathe a timeless spell.
Scales shine bright in the moon's soft light,
Secrets dance and take their flight.

Beneath the rocks, where silence reigns,
Echoes murmur of forgotten gains.
Old tales spun in a silvery thread,
Reverberate for the lost and dead.

Glimmers of gold in the dusky air,
Hints of magic linger everywhere.
Creeping vines hold close the past,
In the hollow where spells are cast.

Ancient eyes watch from afar,
Guiding dreams like a falling star.
The flicker of hope in the darkness deep,
In the scaled hollow, secrets keep.

With every breath, the legends rise,
In a world painted with unseen skies.
In the heart of the earth, shadows do play,
In the scaled hollow, night meets day.

The Flicker Within the Fiery Dark

Amidst the shadows, embers glow,
A flicker stirs, a spark to show.
In fiery dark, a tale unfolds,
Of whispered dreams and hearts so bold.

The nightingale sings of worlds unseen,
While echoes hum in the spaces in between.
With every flicker, the spirits wake,
In a dance of light, the memories quake.

The flames, they twist like tales of yore,
Kindling hope on a distant shore.
Through the darkness, bright visions chase,
In the fiery dark, hold your place.

With wands like candles, we weave our fate,
Within the glow, we hesitate.
For in the flicker, courage found,
And in our hearts, the magic's bound.

So let the light be a guiding spark,
In the vastness of the fiery dark.
For those who dream and dare to rise,
The flicker holds the brightest skies.

The Wizard's Lament for Faded Spells

In shadows deep, a wizard grieves,
For spells once bright, now faded leaves.
With wand in hand, he weaves a sigh,
For magic lost beneath the sky.

The cauldron bubbles, yet silence reigns,
In echoing halls of unspoken pains.
What once brought joy now brings despair,
Faded spells hang heavy in the air.

Through parchment dust and cobweb threads,
He clings to dreams of warmth that spreads.
With every memory, a heart's ache,
A wizard's lament, a fragile wake.

Alchemical keys rust in the night,
Locked away from the flickering light.
Once fierce and free, his heart now quelled,
In the depths of a world where hope rebelled.

Yet in the quiet, a shimmer glows,
A chance to mend what fate bestows.
In the darkest hour, he holds a spark,
A wizard's heart ignites the dark.

Songs of the Ancients Forgotten

In the twilight, the ancients hum,
Songs of wisdom, they softly strum.
From the stones, their voices rise,
Echoes trapped in the endless skies.

Memories float on a gentle breeze,
Tales of glory among the trees.
With every note, the past awakes,
In chords of longing, the heart partakes.

The stars listen with gleaming eyes,
As the songs of ancients fill the skies.
In whispers tender and soft as night,
The love of ages takes to flight.

Through rocky crags and forests wide,
The ancient songs will ever abide.
History's echo, forever played,
In the heart of nature, the music stayed.

So dance to the tune that time forgot,
In every heartbeat, hear what is sought.
For songs of old, though whisper thin,
In silence, joy and sorrow spin.

Flickering Echoes of the Eldritch Chamber

In shadows deep where whispers dwell,
Ancient tales weave a binding spell.
A flicker bright, a ghostly light,
Guides the lost through endless night.

Beneath the stone, a heartbeat thrums,
Calling forth the silent drums.
Secrets held in ivy's grasp,
Awaiting fate's embracing clasp.

The torchlight dances, forms appear,
Echoes soft that we must hear.
Through timeworn halls, the stories flow,
Of battles fought and truths we know.

A shiver runs as phantoms sigh,
In every breath, a reason why.
In silence thick, the past unfolds,
A tapestry of dreams and holds.

The chamber breathes with every soul,
Unearth your heart, embrace the whole.
With every flicker, understand,
The echoes bridge the worlds at hand.

Forgotten Wishes in the Dragon's Shadow

Beneath the wings of ancient pride,
Whispers echo, hopes collide.
A treasure lost in time's embrace,
A wish forgotten, holds its place.

In dragon's shadow, secrets hide,
Flickering flames where dreams reside.
A memory wrapped in starlit thread,
Awakens longings once thought dead.

Softly, softly, the night unfolds,
Carrying stories that time upholds.
Magic swirls in twilight's breath,
Among the living, and those of death.

With every heartbeat, a promise clings,
To skies where hope on dragon's wings.
Forgotten wishes, bright as day,
Will find their course, will find their way.

So lift your gaze unto the skies,
For every wish has wings to rise.
In shadows deep, let courage shine,
For in the dark, your dreams align.

Dim Reflections of a Shattered Dream

In mirrored glass where echoes clash,
Dreams collide in a fleeting flash.
What once was whole, now lies in shards,
Each jagged piece a tale that guards.

The night reflects a sorrow's song,
Dimmed by whispers of what went wrong.
Shadows of joy entwined in fear,
In broken dreams, our truths appear.

With every flicker, hope ignites,
Casting light on long-lost sights.
For now we know the weight we bear,
Is but a testament of care.

Through shattered glass, a path remains,
To find the beauty in our pains.
In dim reflections, we uncover,
The strength within, the heart's true lover.

So gather courage, brave the night,
For dreams reborn will take their flight.
In fragments lie a story grand,
The shattered dream, a guiding hand.

Embers Kissing the Edge of Eternity

In twilight's breath, the embers glow,
Kissing the edge where moments flow.
Time weaves slowly, yet fierce it burns,
As hearts entwined find their returns.

Each flicker tells a tale of old,
Of love and loss, of brave and bold.
In twilight's dance, we learn to see,
Eternity in what could be.

The stars above, like lanterns bright,
Guide us through the velvet night.
Embers whisper, soft and clear,
The promise held when hope is near.

Let not the shadows dim your flame,
For every spark calls out your name.
Embers kissed by time's gentle hand,
Yearn to light the dreamer's land.

So breathe the fire, embrace the spark,
Find warmth and love within the dark.
As embers kiss the edge of fate,
In every heartbeat, we create.

Lost Wonders Among the Shadows

In chambers deep where whispers dwell,
Forgotten tales of magic swell.
Each shadow holds a secret thrum,
Of heroes past and battles won.

With flickering lights that softly sway,
The echoes dance, they twist, they play.
A tapestry of lost delight,
In moonlit hues, the stars ignite.

Of ancient paths where footsteps fade,
In forest glades, their glories laid.
The roots below, entwined in dreams,
Each silence holds a thousand screams.

Amidst the night, a lantern glows,
A beacon for what no one knows.
Yet in these shades, hope's whispers found,
In murmurs soft, life's pulse is sound.

Oh, lost wonders of yesteryear,
Amidst the dark, your voice we hear.
In every heart, in every song,
The magic lives, forever strong.

The Ashen Tapestry of Ages

Upon the loom of time it weaves,
A tapestry of long-lost leaves.
With threads of ash and whispers low,
The stories of the ages flow.

Each hue reflects a moment past,
In muted tones, reflections cast.
The fate of worlds in silken seams,
A blend of shadows, hopes, and dreams.

Embers glow within the gray,
Of destinies that shaped the day.
A flicker here, a shimmer there,
In every stitch, a soul laid bare.

In twilight's grip, the fabric bends,
The threads of suffering, joy transcends.
With every knot, a tale unfolds,
Of fleeting moments, brave and bold.

Thus, on this loom, all fates entwined,
In every line, a heart aligned.
The ashen hues, their strength is found,
In whispered dreams that wrap around.

Veils of Mystique in the Serpent's Keep

In winding paths where serpents glide,
The secrets of the night abide.
Beneath the moon, in shadows deep,
Lie veils of mystique, silence keeps.

A fortress bound by ancient lore,
With echoes from the days of yore.
The chill of dusk, a shivering stone,
Holds stories whispered, dreams alone.

A flicker bright, a fleeting glare,
In hidden corners, hiding there.
A mage's heart, a lover's sigh,
In every breath, a wish to fly.

The serpent coils, in waiting still,
A guardian of each fated thrill.
With scales that shimmer, shadows dance,
In every heart, a daring chance.

Oh, veils of mystique, ever true,
In night's embrace, we find the hue.
Of magic's breath, both wild and sweet,
In the serpent's keep, our souls shall meet.

Dreams Entwined with Smoke

In realms where phantoms weave and twine,
Dreams entwined in ribbons fine.
With tendrils dark that fade away,
A dance of shadows, night and day.

The clouds of thought like wisps of air,
Float softly here, as if in prayer.
Each wish a flicker, a spark ignites,
In smoky trails, the heart's delights.

With whispered tones, the visions grow,
In swirling mists, where rivers flow.
A tapestry of hope and fear,
Each moment lived, crystal clear.

In twilight's haze, the dreams arise,
In soft embrace, beneath the skies.
They flicker bright then softly fade,
In every heart, a serenade.

So chase the smoke, let visions soar,
In every dream, there lies much more.
In fleeting moments, life awakes,
The dreams we weave, the paths we take.

9 781805 644194